Adversity and Awakening

by Sri Swami Satchidananda

Library of Congress Cataloging in
Publication Data
Satchidananda, Swami.

Adversity and Awakening

ISBN: 978-0-932040-68-8

Printed in the United States of America.

Integral Yoga® Publications
Satchidananda Ashram–Yogaville, Inc.
108 Yogaville Way, Buckingham, VA, USA 23921
www.YogaAndPeace.org

Yogaville, Virginia, USA

Books by
Sri Swami Satchidananda

Beyond Words

Bound To Be Free:
The Liberating Power
of Prison Yoga

Enlightening Tales

The Golden Present

The Healthy Vegetarian

Heaven on Earth

Integral Yoga Hatha

Kailash Journal

The Living Gita

To Know Your Self

Yoga Sutras of Patanjali

Titles in this special
Peter Max cover art series:

Meditation

The Key to Peace

Overcoming Obstacles

Adversity and Awakening

Satchidananda Sutras

Gems of Wisdom

Pathways to Peace

How to Find Happiness

The Be-Attitudes

Everything Will Come to You

Thou Art That:
How to Know Yourself

Free Yourself

The Guru Within

Books / Films about
Sri Swami Satchidananda

Sri Swami Satchidananda:
  Biography of a Yoga Master

Sri Swami Satchidananda:
  Portrait of a Modern Sage

Boundless Giving: The Life and Service of
Sri Swami Satchidananda

The Master's Touch

Living Yoga: The life and teachings of
  Swami Satchidananda (DVD)

Many Paths, One Truth: The Interfaith
  Message of Swami Satchidananda (DVD)

The Essence of Yoga:
  The Path of Integral Yoga with
  Swami Satchidananda (DVD)

For complete listing of books, CDs and DVDs:
www.iydbooks.com

Contents

The Nature of Suffering

Again and again, people ask me, "Why is there suffering? How can I avoid suffering?" My answer is, "You cannot."

Knowing the purpose and the meaning of suffering itself is an answer to suffering. Once you know that suffering is for your benefit, you won't have to be worried about it. You won't suffer for that. You will gladly go through it. Don't think that Nature or anybody is interested in causing you suffering. Our suffering is the way to clean out our problems. There's no gentle way.

If linen is dirty it has to go through suffering in the laundromat. You can't expect the laundryman to fold it, put it on the altar, burn some incense and say, "Get clean." No. The cloth has to go through suffering, washing and drying; then it's nice and clean. So that's what. Suffering is the effort that goes into cleaning out the problems. The suffering increases if you resist it, if you don't understand its purpose.

That's why Mother Nature herself is a factory. We are all being rubbed and scrubbed and chiseled and cut and filed until we are fit for the showroom–like a piece of marble that becomes a beautiful statue that is put on the altar and worshipped. Life is like that. So if we understand this well, we will accept all the adversities and suffering. We will thank the people who bring us sufferings. Why? They are messengers of God.

When somebody comes and brings you some suffering, know that God has sent that person out of kindness. Accept it. The great advantage in this attitude is that you keep your peace and you don't create negative feelings. Because the moment you create negative feelings, you lose your peace.

So, have faith and know, "God is doing it for my benefit." Whatever you cannot control, leave it to God. Whenever you're able to correct a problem by yourself, take care of it. Beyond that, offer it to God: "It's all Yours."

How to Find Peace and Joy in a Chaotic World

How do we find peace and joy in the middle of a chaotic world? In the midst of the chaos, find the balance, and then you find the peace. When are you peaceful? When there is nothing to disturb your peace? That is not the true test of real inner peace. When there's everything to disturb your peace, that's the most important time to be peaceful.

In the midst of chaos, troubles, terrorism and disasters, that's when you want to be peaceful. If there were no problems, if everybody could be peaceful, then why would you need something like Yoga? In the face of any and all problems, you should find peace. It's worth it, and you can do it.

Peace of mind is the greatest treasure in the world. All the rest is nothing if you don't have peace of mind. Sometimes, even in the name of saving the world, we lose our peace of mind. You might stand on a platform and shout, "Hey, I have a way to save the world. Come, listen to me." If nobody comes, then you will get disappointed. In that case, you want to spread peace, but you lose your peace. If there's one great treasure in the world that's worth seeking, it is peace of mind. All other things are nothing compared to this.

Once you get that peace of mind, all the rest–people, material things, name, fame, everything–will follow automatically because you are a peaceful person. They will love to be with you if you are peaceful and if you don't run after them. If you find peace within yourself, you will find peace everywhere. It starts from within you. You're not going to find peace outside if you don't have it yourself. We say, "Charity begins at home." I would say, "Everything begins at home."

What you have inside, you will see outside. If your eyes are jaundiced, what will you see? Yellow everywhere. You might ask, "How come everyone is wearing yellow clothes today?" Are they all really wearing yellow today? No. Why do you see yellow? Because your eyes are jaundiced. If your eyes are clean, you can see everything clearly. So, correct yourself first. Whatever you want to see outside in the world, find it first within yourself.

If there is another word for God, I would say it is peace. You have peace always in you, as your True Nature. God is peace and God is in you as peace. The Kingdom of God is within you. If you really experience peace mentally—complete peace, serenity and tranquility—then you are actually experiencing God. You are in God when you are in peace.

The moment you disturb your peace, you seem to miss that God. So to find God, what you need is a peaceful and tranquil mind. Your mind should not be agitated in any way. If you lose your peace, you lose everything. If you have peace, you have everything. Whatever happens, don't lose your peace. Maintain your peace at all costs. When I say "at all costs" I mean that. You can give up everything and anything but not your peace. Your first and foremost duty is to make sure that the mind does not lose its peace.

Treasure the peace of your mind so much that nothing, nothing, nothing can shake your peace. Everything else is nothing compared to peace of mind. You should be ready to renounce whatever stands in the way of retaining your peace. What good is it to have the whole world and no peace in your heart?

You don't have to make the mind peaceful. It is already peaceful. If at times you seem to have lost your peace, it's not that peace left you, but you simply disturbed it. Many times people ask this question: "How can I find peace?" The answer is, "You don't have to go and find it; you have it. Please don't disturb it." We should take care that we don't lose our peace due to our thoughts, words or actions.

Whatever comes and whatever goes, it doesn't matter. Don't lose your peace. By being peaceful yourself, you can inspire others to be peaceful. You don't have to bring peace to the whole world. Bring peace to the place where you are sitting. If you are peaceful, at least that part of the world is peaceful. Is it not so? Do it first. Then you can think of others. Your most important and very first responsibility is to maintain your peace. Without that, even if you take action to help others, you're not going to do it well. You can be useful only when you are easeful and peaceful. If you lose your ease and peace, you become a nuisance to others.

Don't get caught in these ups and downs in life. Life is filled with ups and downs. We say sometimes, "One day we will have a peaceful world." People ask me, "Will there be any time when the whole world will be peaceful?" My answer is, "Sorry, it won't be." That may disappoint people; but the world can never be peaceful always. No. The world is always filled with dualities—ups and downs, day and night, right and left and so on. The opposites are part of the nature. But you can still find peace.

My advice is to see that you maintain your peace under all situations. Do you want to know the secret to peace? Say, "God, I am Thine, all is Thine. Thy will be done." That is the secret of my peace. When you accept God's will, then you can retain your peace. And then, with the retention of your peace, you can play your part well in life. What is better than a peaceful life? Peace and happiness go together. Those who live in peace, live in joy.

Faith and Fear Do Not Go Together

Faith and fear do not go together. When you have faith in God you leave everything in God's hands. If you are afraid of anything, I have to doubt your faith. Have absolute faith, absolute faith. Blessed are the pure in heart; they shall have faith, and they shall see God. If you have absolute purity of heart, it's there you can find this faith and find God. In a way, we could say that faith is more than God; because it's your faith that makes God. That kind of faith can come only in a child-like, clean, pure heart. Remember that if you have absolute faith, nothing, nothing is impossible. You can get healed. The real incurable disease is faithlessness.

We acquire faith only through suffering. Only then do you realize that nothing in this world is going to bring you eternal happiness and peace. Then, you can say, "I tried this and that; I ran here and there, but I ran into troubles everywhere." When we really understand the world and its nature, we stop seeking external happiness and turn to God. Then our faith becomes really strong. When you suffer, do you think God is trying to hurt you or do something damaging to you? No, God has a purpose. God might have said, "Because they won't learn lessons easily, let me put them into some situation where they will suffer. Then, through the suffering, let them learn the lesson." My Master, Swami Sivanandaji used to say, "Pain is your friend." We even have the expression: "No pain, no gain." So if you want a gain, you have to accept the pain.

Don't blame God for that. On the other hand, praise God for sending the lesson. "God, thanks, You gave me suffering. Through that experience, I'm getting cleaned." To clean up anything, you have to put it through suffering, sometimes a lot of suffering. It's just as simple as cleaning a cloth or a shirt. How much suffering does the cloth go through to get cleaned? Don't hesitate to welcome suffering if you're interested in that gain. That's the advantage of going through pain in life, going through suffering in life. We have to make mistakes to learn the correct way. So, the secret of life is accepting suffering and then learning the lesson.

Total surrender and total faith alone will take care of many things. Lord Jesus told his followers he would carry their burdens. Lord Krishna assured his devotees that, if they surrendered themselves to him, he would take care of all their problems. God is promising us that. God doesn't have to promise, but still says, "I promise you," because God knows the human mind. However much God says this, we don't believe it. So God says, "I promise you I will take care of you if you leave everything to Me." But our egos seldom allow us to do this. When you try everything and everything fails, then you come back to God.

Anybody who has that complete faith in God will be freed from all their problems. God is alive and is nearer to you than your own heart. God is in you, outside of you. Every minute God knows what you are thinking, what you mean when you say something. All that God expects is a pure heart, that of a baby. Like a baby totally in the hands of the mother, surrender yourself to God.

Look at all these sages and saints, they didn't lose anything by surrendering themselves to God. They lived a life of total surrender, relying on God. They show us the way. They have said it. They can only show the way, but they can't make us do it. Similarly, you can take the horse to water, but you can't make it drink. We have to do it ourselves. If you have an ounce of faith you can move mountains–that's what the *Bible* promises you.

We may talk a lot about "faith, faith, faith." You can easily hear a lot about that. But true faith comes only through your own ordeals. It's easy to say, "Oh, of course I have faith in God." But, what if God doesn't give you the outcome you expected from an important situation? What if the outcome is a huge disappointment? If, instead of accepting that, you get terribly upset, that is conditional faith. God wants unconditional faith.

Know that such faith does not come that easily. When we stop running away from pain and suffering, then we turn to God. It's at that time our faith becomes stronger. And God waits until that time also. God isn't in a hurry to come and save us. God says, "I will wait. When you have had enough you will come to me, I know."

Don't put your faith in fear. Put your faith in God. Have complete faith. Don't even go near fear. Remember: If anything has to happen, it will happen. Think, "All right, let it happen. I am bold. What's the use of being afraid of it? I'm not going to be able to stop anything that is meant to happen." If you really have faith, you don't have to be afraid of anything. That doesn't mean that you should not be careful. Be careful, but don't be afraid.

Facing Death and Loss

When people are facing very serious illness or great loss, they often ask me, "How can I still have faith?" My answer is, "Keep the faith." All medical treatments work better if you have faith. Does fear ever help you? No. On the other hand the fear makes you feel worse. It puts more poison in your system. So, don't lose your faith. When faith is lost, everything is lost. If you don't have faith in your doctor, even if he or she gives you healing nectar, I doubt that it will work for you. So, it's not the doctor or the medicine; it's your faith that is the most important. My main point here is: Never, never, never lose faith–under any condition, any situation. Keep up that faith; and, then, do whatever you should, whatever you can to take care of the situation.

Even with strong faith, it may happen that some will not be cured or will even lose their lives. But, if this happens, remember that the life is not lost. Only the body is lost. The life is immortal. There's a big problem when people don't believe in the afterlife. They say, "Oh, this is it, finished." That's another big reason why someone might lose faith–he or she thinks that when someone dies that is the end.

We have to understand that the soul is immortal. Nobody can destroy it. In a way, everything is immortal; everything is filled with life. There's no dead matter in the entire universe. God created everything, is it not so? Is God alive or dead? Alive. And God created everything in God's image. So how can a live God, a living God, create dead matter? If God is alive, everything is alive.

Then what is it that we call "death, death, death?" Change of form, change of name. Somewhere in the forest there is a tree. When the tree dies, it's no longer there; but, now, you use the tree's lumber as rafters and beams to build your house. The tree dies, and the rafter is born. A piece of cloth dies, a nice robe is born. Firewood dies, ash is born. Food dies when it goes into the stomach and energy is born. So, what does that mean? It only changes from one form into another form. The essence is the same; it's always there. When it changes its shape, you give it a new name. You might say, "It used to be a piece of cloth; but, now, the shirt is born."

Likewise, the body that has been left by the soul isn't really dead. Living particles from the cosmos were gathered to make the body; and, when the time comes, the composed body decomposes and separates. Then, the particles go back to their source; in between, the particles may have different names and forms. As such, everything has that immortal soul. We never die. And remember that you are not that body or those particles that made it. We are all eternal because we are the image of that eternal God.

The only thing in life that is certain is change. If we believe that everything that happens in our lives is for our highest good, then we will have more peace. If you see everything as God's story, why should you worry about anything? It's all God's—pleasure, pain, profit, loss—everything is God's. The world is a mixture of ups and downs. If there is one, there is going to be the other.

The major cause of worry is the loss of people or material things in our lives. You may have lost someone or some thing. But don't lose something else: your peace of mind. With the proper understanding you will realize you never came with anything and you are not going to go with anything. It's the mind that wants to cling to things, to possess things. As pure Self you don't own anything. You utilize things in order to serve well. We come empty-handed and go empty-handed. In the meantime, if things come, enjoy them. Things are simply loaned for our use, they are not ours to possess. And if they go, accept that also. Realize there must be a good reason; because what we need will always be provided. But remember: What you need will be provided, not necessarily what you want.

It's the same with the loss of loved ones. Do they belong to us? Can we possess them? Can we take them with us when we go? Life is like a journey. In between birth and death, many people come into our lives. They are all our fellow travelers and teachers. Don't we often meet people in a plane or on a train? You may say hello to each other, sit together for a while, until the destination of one person is reached. Then you say, "Bye, bye; see you later." We are all on a journey, and we each have different stops we make along the way.

Death is nothing but changing the forms. One changes into another, so the old one dies and a new form is born. Take, for example, a chair: it was a tree before. The tree died; the chair was born. Birth and death are like that. All we can do is to pray for the soul's journey. Let the soul go wherever it wants; ultimately it will reach God. That's how we have to accept death.

It's all right to mourn the death of the body. But, we also have to accept the inevitable. Everything that is born will eventually die. Still, you do love that soul. So, if you're feeling sad, pray for that soul. That's the best way to help that soul. If you still love that soul, pray for that soul. "May that soul be at God's feet or in a higher place and find peace and comfort." You can also help the soul by letting go of your grief as much as possible, and as soon as possible.

Sometimes when you grieve, you bring more sadness to that soul–because that soul watches us. Even though the body is no longer there, the soul can still watch you, at least for some time. If that particular soul is attached to you, he or she will be watching you. When you grieve, the soul becomes unhappy, thinking, "I am free now. I am running around, moving freely. I am happy; but, in my name, my loved one is sad." Why are we sad? Because we don't have that person in the physical body among us. It's for our selfish reason that we feel sad. Then, you make that soul sad by your unhappiness.

When the soul leaves the body, it's a release from the prison, the body prison. You ought to be happy about it. If you can't be happy, at least pray for their soul; don't feel sad about it. That's not going to help anybody—neither that soul nor your soul. Physical death is not the culmination of the soul's journey. The *Bhagavad Gita* says that the Self is eternal. The body may die, but the soul never dies because the soul is part of God. We come into a body and we live in the body; it's like a recreational vehicle. When the body gets into an accident, or, because of illness, the body isn't good anymore, the soul leaves the body to take another body. Then it continues its journey.

Nature and Natural Disasters

Nothing, nothing, nothing moves without God's will. We are sad when calamities happen, but who could stop them? Whom would you blame for it? It's God's or Nature's act. It's all God's will. Ultimately, that is the truth. All God's will. Creation, preservation, destruction. One without the other is impossible. Unless you destroy you cannot create again. Nature composed all things; and, in their own time all things will decompose. People, plants, animals, landscapes–all things have their own time. No one can ever stop it. So, learn to accept Nature's law.

Sometimes the scientists can tell us, "A hurricane is coming." With scientific readings they may find out, even ahead of time, that there is going to be a hurricane. All right; you evacuate the people. That's good. I'm not saying you shouldn't do that. Do it. But don't think that by doing this you become eternal. In the middle of all this creation, preservation and destruction there's one thing that is never created, never preserved, never destroyed–one thing that is eternal. That is the Spirit.

On the human level we can say that is the *Atma*, or the soul. The soul was not created. It is there, it was there; it is here, and it will be ever immortal. The immortal principle. But it takes different forms. When it takes a new form, you call it a birth. It stays for awhile; and, when, the form is broken–it dies. When suffering comes from Nature itself, that also teaches us. These kinds of situations help us learn to live as a global family. We remember that this is God's home and we are all children of God. We are one family. With that understanding, we will collectively take care of each other and the world. Even if one individual is unhappy, everybody will take care of that person and see that he or she becomes happy again.

So, when calamities occur, try to do something. That doesn't mean you have to help the whole world. You didn't create the world, and you're not going to save the world. Every one of us has limited responsibility. We do whatever we can, within our capacity. Leave the rest to the One who created the world.

Terrorism

We hear so much about terrorist attacks all over the globe. These attacks are a sad thing, no doubt. For the sake of everybody, you can express your sadness, but don't let yourself actually become depressed. If you get depressed, you can't do anything useful. Look at all those terrible things that happened on 9/11 and how all those rescue personnel went there to find the bodies, who each victim was, where they lived. The doctors went there to take care of the survivors; but, if they had gotten upset over these things, they couldn't even have done their jobs. They had to keep their emotions under control and do what was necessary.

I admire those people. It's not that they weren't saddened–they were, no doubt. But, they didn't allow themselves to be affected by it. If they were overcome with emotions, they would have added to the problem. Suppose a patient faints and you call the doctor, a compassionate doctor. He or she sees the patient; then the doctor faints! Then you have to call another doctor for two patients! So, to really serve well, you need to keep yourself in control.

Of course, we all want to understand why this is happening and what we can do to help the situation. What else can we do? Pray and take every opportunity to serve people. Offer your services in any way you can. Many people suffer because of these adversities. When you see those families who have lost their relatives, offer them some kind words of consolation.

When Nature strikes or when terrorist attacks take place, there are soon lots of people standing in lines at hospitals to donate blood. Extend yourself in whatever way you can—by kind words, by service, by money—because these are times to think of others and to do whatever we can to help relieve suffering. Prayer and service to the needy is what you can do right now. So pray and serve, but don't let your mind be clouded by worry.

We also have to realize that God is giving us a big wake-up call. Had we ever before seen the entire Congress, without any partisan animosity, standing together and praying as they did after 9/11? What made that happen? If not for that terrible calamity, they wouldn't be coming together like that. And it's not just in the political arena. What a great interfaith prayer meeting was held at the National Cathedral. So many people offered their very lives trying to save others at Ground Zero. They all forgot themselves as individuals and worked for the common good. We really have paid a big price to learn this lesson.

All these kinds of calamities make us come together. They force us to remember God and to unite as one family, regardless of our faiths and backgrounds. They make us remember how we are all the same, how we need one another. People are going back to their own churches as well as meeting with people of different faiths. There is a huge surge in interfaith services all over the country. People who wouldn't even talk together before are praying together, working together, seeing and serving the common humanity.

If we could live that way always, certainly we would have a heaven right here on earth. That's exactly what yogic life means: living a collective life and rising above selfishness, sharing the joy of everyone and the pain of everyone. Let us learn that first—to love and give, care and share. Then, we will really see a beautiful heaven on this earth.

The Law of Karma

As spiritual seekers, we should understand that, while we may not know exactly how or why disasters and tragedies happen, they happen for a purpose. That's where the law of karma comes in. Karma is the law of cause and effect. What we sow, we reap at one time or another. When disaster strikes a country as we saw with 9/11, it means that we may have some karma as a country that we are now facing. Nothing happens to us without our karma.

Karma is a word that is often used casually, but many people don't understand what it really means. The Sanskrit term karma can mean two things: action, and also, the result of action. So, when you do karma (an action) you reap karma (the resulting action). Every action will leave its result; every cause will bear its effect. No action goes without its reaction.

There are three levels of karma: Those being expressed and exhausted through this birth (*prarabda* karma); new karmas being created during this birth (*agami* karma); and those waiting to be fulfilled in future births (*sanjita* karma). For example, if you purposely go and kick a stone and hurt your toe, that's *agami* karma. If you're just walking around and all of a sudden hit a stone and get hurt, that's due to *prarabda*. We control the second two stages of karmas, but we can't do anything about the *prarabda* karma; we just have to accept it.

These karmas are something like the equipment of an archer. He or she has a number of arrows in the arrow holder. The arrows would then be in three different stages. Once having shot an arrow, it has already left the bow and is on its way to its target (*prarabda* karma). You have no more control over it. You can neither stop it now nor draw it back. As long you stay in this body, the karma allotted to this birth will continue. If you draw an arrow from the quiver, put it in the bow and aim it, it is like a new karma you're creating now (*agami* karma). You have full control over it. If you want, you can keep those arrows in the quiver (*sanjita* karma). Otherwise, you can take them out. It's in your hands.

The good and bad, the pleasure and pain that you enjoy is not given to you by anybody else. You sowed it; you are reaping it. If you sow a bitter seed, you will have a bitter fruit. If that's clearly understood, then that itself is a big relief from the suffering. Because the moment you know that your suffering is there to clean you up, it's no longer suffering. We have to purge out our karma. It's almost like, without knowing it, you ate something wrong. Now, it's creating a problem, and you're throwing it up. That may not be pleasant, but it will get what is harmful out of your system.

All our pains are like that. If you understand the pain, it's no longer a pain; it's a blessing because it's helping you. If you have to undergo surgery, you will pay thousands of dollars to the doctors to perform an operation, to even chop off parts of the body if it's necessary to save your life. Do you refuse? No. Why not? Because you know that you can't survive without the operation.

If you sow something, somebody else can't reap it. Action and reaction. Your life and its fruit. It comes to you whether you want it or not. Nothing happens to us without our karma. So, we have to purge out our karma. When we don't think of that, we simply blame others. "Oh, that person is the cause of my problems." That's very wrong thinking. As spiritual seekers we should know that whatever happens in our personal life– or in public life–is God's will. Without God's will, not even an atom can move.

It's very difficult to make sense of such tragedies as earthquakes, tsunamis or terrorist attacks. But, as yogis, we should understand that, although we may not know exactly how or why these things happen, they happen for a reason and with a purpose.

Let us remember that adversities are blessings in disguise. If we look only at the adversities, we'll be consumed with sorrow, fear and despair. That will not help during these times. Rather, it's better to remember that there's a purpose behind everything. Ultimately, everything that happens is God's will. God, or the Universal Cosmic Power, is making us remember that it's all God's will and it's all for good and that's for certain.

Despondency and Suicide
Won't Bring Relief

When suffering comes, face it. Don't cop out. The suffering may feel unbearable, but you must bear it. You cannot escape from karma. Committing suicide only adds more karma. Then, your suffering will be multiplied. You cannot put an end to your unhappiness this way, so instead say: "Whatever it is, I'll be strong enough to face it." Purge out your karma.

Suicide is not permitted in any faith. Suicide is against God's will. When Nature wants us to live, if we put forth an effort of our own to oppose that force, we will have to be punished in a greater way for that crime. So, people who commit suicide are really not going to escape from anything; they'll be paying a greater toll later on.

You think that by committing suicide you can save yourself from the problem; but it's not so. It's almost like riding in a car that is speeding along; all of a sudden you decide that you don't want to be in that car, so you jump out. But it creates more problems. And then you realize that it's too late.

At the time of death, we simply drop the physical body. The spirit doesn't stay in the body; it leaves. When a person leaves the body prematurely—not by a natural death but because of suicide—that soul needs another body. The soul's karma in that particular body is interrupted, and this leaves the soul stranded.

A normal death, even if from an accident, would be like arranging to move—you arrange some other apartment somewhere and you vacate this apartment. That is normal death. You have enough time to transfer your things, go and settle there in your new home.

This body is your house, your dwelling place. Committing suicide means that, suddenly, you destroy your home. What happens to you then? You become homeless. If you are just driven out of this apartment suddenly, and if you don't have any other apartment to go to, where will you be? You will be on the street, homeless. Like that, with suicide, you will be bodiless. The body is a home. Until you get another body you will become bodiless and you will have to roam about.

Let me give one other example: committing suicide is something like being angry with your car because the engine won't start. You take a sledge hammer to the car, breaking it apart. Then, after it's too late, you suddenly realize: "Oh, what am I to do? I don't have a car!"

If you consciously and willfully destroy your body, then, after you lose the body, you'll realize–too late–that you shouldn't have done that. You get stranded and then you look for a body. The spirit may go in search of a vehicle in order to fulfill its journey. It tries to possess a vehicle–someone else's living body.

People who commit suicide lose the body that was given to them to be able to purge their karma. Without a proper transition, they run around without a body, as astral elements. They wanted to commit suicide to escape from something, but really there's no escape. It's better to accept the situation and face it.

Suicide is the worst thing someone could do. The soul that leaves the body that way will be much more miserable and will cause others, who have been left behind, to face misery. That's why committing suicide is the worst karma. It neither benefits you nor others. So, one has to accept, "Whatever suffering comes, I will accept it, face it bravely and purge out this karma."

Why Anger Won't Help Us

If we don't accept our karma, then all we'll have is anger and animosity in our hearts. That will certainly not help us in any way. Will our anger and hatred bring back loved ones? Will it bring peace to our world? No. So, the first thing is to root out any anger or desire for vengeance from our hearts and pray for all the suffering souls, and even for those who seem to be at fault in these terrible situations.

How can we pray for those who do hurt us? Remember what Jesus said: "Forgive them, for they know not what they do." If they really understood what they were doing, they wouldn't do it. That doesn't mean they shouldn't be brought to justice; they should be. But, we should understand that their minds are confused. As yogis we need a deeper understanding and broader perspective when viewing what is happening in our world.

If we focus only on the negative, we become filled with fear and anxiety, or anger and hatred. A yogi, on the other hand, will look upon everything with equanimity and balance. This may sound too detached; but, if you harbor anger and hatred, you're adding more fuel to the fire and you aren't doing anything to heal or help anyone.

On the other hand, these negative feelings are going to make you suffer first. You hurt yourself by your angry words or thoughts of hatred or despair. Because, as we all know, you are what you think. If you think well, you will be well. If you think ill, you will be ill.

Before you hurt others by your anger and hatred, you hurt yourself. It's not worth it. Of course, if our minds are not under our control, immediately the anger will come. At least those people who are involved in spiritual practices should train their minds. Otherwise, the mind will not help us and we will not help anybody else either.

In the case of terrorists or people who commit wrong acts, we need clear, balanced minds in order to punish the culprits for their mistakes. We don't hate them; we needn't even be angry with them. It's almost like in a classroom when a child makes some mistake and the teacher corrects him or her. Does the teacher hate the child? No. He or she is correcting the child out of love.

Anger is good if you can keep it in your pocket. Use it when you want to make a point or take charge of a situation, but don't actually get angry. It's like acting–you appear angry without actually becoming angry–you remain balanced and in control. And, that's what should happen with regard to terrorism, also. The leaders of governments, instead of getting angry, can use punishment to correct the situation. There's nothing wrong with that, and it will have a positive effect. When used this way, getting angry is not negative; it could be positive.

You have to show anger in certain situations, in order to create a positive effect. But, you have to know how to use it. That means, you have to control your mind. You have to be master of your own mind. The greatest victory you can win is over your own mind. That's what Yoga is all about.

Religion Doesn't Teach
Hatred and Killing

This is a time for us to remember that in the name of religion more people have been killed than in all the wars and natural calamities put together. Now, more than ever, we must understand that the purpose of religion is not to separate us. True faiths don't teach hatred and killing, nor did any of the prophets. It's the people who wrongly interpret the scriptures who create the divisions. Division comes if we put our egos into the teachings of these religions. Let us strive to be free of that kind of egoism.

Some terrorists say they do these terrible acts for God and in the name of God. God did not ask them to do this. Even the scriptures, the words of sages and saints, are understood through one's own mind. We interpret everything the way we want, depending on the state of our minds. Allah or Muhammad or Jesus or Moses or Shankara never recommended this kind of violence. Even when they used different words, they taught, "Love your neighbor as yourself." However, some people are not ready to accept that, and they interpret the scriptures in distorted ways.

Here is a story to illustrate this point: Once upon a time, there was a condemned prisoner who had been sentenced to death and was about to be hanged. Right at that moment, a message came to the authorities in the form of a telegram. Unfortunately, there was no punctuation in the telegram.

One of the authorities read: "HANG HIM. NOT LET HIM GO."

Another one of the authorities, who had a kind heart, who was sorry for this man, said:

"We are ready to hang him; why should they have sent such a message? There is something wrong with that. Let me read it."

He read the telegram like this: "HANG HIM NOT. LET HIM GO.'"

Each person read the same message from his own perspective. That is how "interpretation" occurs. And, that is why we have "Holy" Crusades and Jihad. In the name of God, some wrongly interpret scriptures as saying, "Kill people." No. God didn't want it, and the sages and saints who gave the teachings never wanted it. If people want to do something evil, they can always quote scriptures as their authority.

What You Can Do

The Hindu scriptures tell us clearly how a *jivanmukta*, a realized liberated soul, would act in any and all circumstances. He or she would not worry about the past: past is past. A *jivanmukta* won't think of the future. Whatever is the present, such a person will see it and accept it. The example given in the Hindu scriptures is that if, during midday, all of a sudden the sun becomes the moon and the cool moonlight shines down on you, will it be a big surprise? For a *jivanmukta* it won't be.

If a *jivanmukta* walks around a graveyard and, all of a sudden, one grave opens up and somebody gets up from the grave and says, "Hello, how are you?" it wouldn't be a surprise to the liberated person. Imagine if something happened like that, how astonished you would be, how shocked you would be. But a *jivanmukta* would just say, "It must be what God wanted."

I'm not making light of shocking tragedies, but I'm just translating a scriptural verse about what a *jivanmukta* is, to help us see what our attitude should be. It says: "The *jivanmukta* will not say, 'This is good; this is bad.' Rather, he or she will say 'It's all God's will.'" By saying that, the *jivanmukta* is simply a witness. Someone like that will just witness everything. The *jivanmukta* can help others without the slightest distraction because there's no disturbance whatsoever in the mind. When you become like that, your service to others in every situation will be the very best. It's not easy; you won't be a *jivanmukta* overnight. So, until you become that kind of *jivanmukta*, do whatever you can to play your part. But, don't become the part. If you become the part, you lose your peace. It may be hard to understand this point, but it's a very important and subtle truth for spiritual seekers.

Life is a drama, and we should play our parts well. What kind of drama is going on in our world, and what part can we play to help? So many people seem to want to help others and our world; yet what can we really do to feel useful during trying times? I say, play your part well. What should we do to play our part? Love and serve. Love and serve all. We were born for that purpose. Don't let yourself get burdened by adversities. Be at ease and do what you can. But, know that you're just playing a part and perform that part with total sincerity. When you play, you should become the part by not becoming it. This may sound like a contradiction, so I will give an example.

Take an actor in a film playing the part of a police officer chasing a criminal. He may appear angry, upset, fierce or even violent. But, if you see the actor walk away after the filming is over, he will just be a normal guy, smiling and calm. While the camera was running, he played. He played because drama is wanted. So, be like that actor: You play the part, but don't become the part. That is important.

If you need to use anger to help a situation, you should look angry. The other fellow should feel you are going to tear him into pieces. But, inside, you know you are not going to do that. This is possible only when you have that good control and mastery over your own mind. Don't get lost in your anger or hatred. For that, you have to train the mind. If you're not well trained, you will get lost in the play. So, learn well, and then go and play your part.

In this world, we never know what's going to happen next. Uncertainty is always there. Nobody knew those terrorists were about to fly into the World Trade Center towers. Nobody knows when hurricanes, flooding, earthquakes or tsunamis will come. Here we are sitting comfortably and in the next moment, who knows? But, that should not stop us from doing what we are doing now. Death can come any minute, in any way. We don't know what's in store for tomorrow, or, whether there will even be a tomorrow. But still, we have the golden present. Now, we are alive and kicking.

Often we take too many responsibilities and burdens on our shoulders. We may think, "Without me the whole world will collapse. I'm the one who must carry the burdens. I'm solely responsible, and I have to take care of everything." It's good to take care of things and lead a responsible life; but you may also be carrying too much on your shoulders, forgetting that you are being carried by Somebody.

Let me tell you a story. There was a man who was going on a trip. He packed two suitcases and went to the river, looking for the boatman to take him across the river to the next village. The boatman looked at this last passenger and his other passengers with their luggage and said, "Well, we have quite a load today; and it may be difficult for my boat to carry all this."

The traveler asked, "The river looks quite calm today, won't it be all right?"

The boatman considered all the factors and told him, "Okay, I think it should be all right."

They set sail, and after they were halfway across, all of a sudden the river started flooding. So, the boatman said, "Uh-oh! I thought the river was quiet and that it would be okay to put in a little extra load. That is why I allowed all of you to get in with so much luggage. But now the boat has become too heavy. You may have to throw out some of your luggage to reduce the weight and save the boat!"

Immediately, everybody started taking their suitcases and throwing them into the water. Everybody, that is, except for the traveler who was the last passenger. The boatman saw that the traveler had lifted his suitcases up and raised them over his head. The boatman shouted, "What are you doing? Throw them out of the boat or we'll all drown!" The traveler exclaimed, "But, they aren't in the boat anymore!" Imagine, he thought he could lighten the load by lifting the suitcases onto his shoulders!

That's what we do very often. That's a sort of subtle ego. Sometimes, we think that way. "I'm stopping the problem. I'm the one to take care of everything. I have to do this to fix it." I don't say that you shouldn't take action. Do it. Just know your limitation. Just do what you can. Like the well-known, wonderful doctors say, "I did all I could. My operation was very successful, but the patient collapsed. What can I do now? I did my job." Leave the rest to God and to karma.

Comforting Those Affected by Disaster

Your mind doesn't have to get unbalanced by adversities, tragedies, disasters, loss and so on. But that doesn't mean you don't care. Show your compassion; show your sadness, outside. With the people who are crying, you have to cry a little, too. That will console them. But you don't really cry inside.

Do you understand what I mean? When you see people crying, you can't say to them: "Oh, it's all for good." No; that won't help at all–it can even hurt. So, express some emotion along with them; that will console them. But, don't let the emotion overwhelm you. That's possible only when you have mastery of your own mind and the right understanding.

All the scriptures have something to help you if you want to bring comfort to those who are suffering. Read the *Bible*, the *Koran*, Sri Patanjali's *Yoga Sutras*, the *Bhagavad Gita*. If they're interested, you can tell them a little about the karma theory. Explain to them that nothing happens to us without our karma. Everything happens because of the karma–action and reaction. So, we have to purge out our karma.

If you have a friend who has lost someone, you can explain with love and compassion that the one who passed away must have purged all his karma and he is probably a free soul now. You miss the body and the personality of your friend. But if you put yourself in the position of that soul, you will know that it would feel, "I'm free now. I'm relieved. I finished all my karma."

The Self, the Soul, can never be dead. It is always alive; because it is part of God. If God made everybody in God's image, how can God die? So, console the friend by saying that the loved one isn't completely lost. She has finished her karma in this body, so she lost the body. She's probably going to have another body if she has yet to undergo some further karma; but, if her karma is finished, she's totally liberated.

And to help your grieving friend understand the situation, you can pray together. I would recommend sharing from the *Bhagavad Gita*, as it talks about the Self and the immortality of the soul. The *Gita* tells us that when the body is gone, it doesn't mean you are gone, as you are neither dead nor born. You are permanent. We go through different bodies. Death is nothing final. Death is as if you take off an old shirt and put on a new one.

How to Pray

I have been asked if there are some special prayers to use during challenging times. I would say to use any prayer that comes from your heart; that is what is most important. You can use your own words to pray for peace for everybody.

The *OM Tryambakam* mantra we repeat in Yogaville and in the Integral Yoga centers is also very good. It's a mantra that helps us to understand the immortality behind all these temporary problems. It goes like this:

> *OM Tryambakam Yajaamahe*
> *Sugandhim Pushti Vardhanam*
> *Urvaarukamiva Bandhanaan*
> *Mrityor Moksheeya Maa Amritaat.*
> *OM Shanti Shanti Shanti.*

The meaning is:

> "We worship the All-Seeing One,
> Fragrant, God nourishes bounteously.
> From the fear of death may God cut us free,
> To realize our immortality.
> OM Peace Peace Peace."

Our prayers will bring benefit, so let us wholeheartedly pray for the world. Let us spend at least a few minutes each day in meditation. To me, those are the most important minutes. You may not even realize the effect, but these peaceful vibrations will help millions of peace-less minds. You'll be helping the whole world find peace and joy. And you can carry this peaceful feeling all through the day, all through the week, all through your life.

Even in the midst of a busy life, you can retain this peace. With this outlook the whole world will become a heaven on earth for you. Every day when you pray, repeat: "May peace, prosperity and happiness be unto all. May all see good in everyone, may all be free from suffering. May the whole world be filled with peace and joy, love and light." When you say this, visualize it, and really feel it. It should be heartfelt if you want to send peaceful energy out into the world.

Of course, we also have to remember that God is not waiting for our prayers. Suppose you pray for somebody. We do that here at Yogaville every day with the repetition of the *OM Tryambakam* mantra. What for? If somebody is sick, we repeat the mantra as if we're asking God, "Please heal that person." Does God not know that the person needs help? Do we have to tell God, "Do this!" before God will take care of the situation? Then, why do we pray? It's not to tell God what to do; it's not even to heal the sick person. It's to bring ourselves into alignment with God and God's healing energy. It's to heal ourselves first.

And, of course, if people know we are all praying for them, they will think, "Oh, so many people are praying for me. I'm sure I will get well." See? You pray, and they listen to that and feel more comfortable and have confidence that they will get well. So, their own confidence helps make them get well. You are helping them to have faith and confidence. You aren't telling God what to do and what not to do. Since that person is also God's child, God is already taking care of him or her. To clean up your own heart, to show how compassionate you are, you're expressing yourself in prayer. It's in this way that prayer helps: It helps you, and it also helps the other person who knows that so many people are praying.

Sometimes, even if you pray for someone's healing, that person won't always get healed. Why? Because God is purging out his or her karma. In Jesus' life, he healed many people, but some people couldn't be healed. Why? If he had that power, he should be able to heal everybody. But he simply offered his prayer. If they were ready to be healed, they would have accepted the prayer and would have been healed. If they were not, their karma wouldn't have allowed the healing; they wouldn't even have accepted healing. So, we do our part without expecting a certain result. Let God do whatever is necessary for that soul.

The Future is Bright

Nobody has control over earthquakes or floods or any natural calamity. Right now we are safe. So, think of today and be happy. Anything can happen tomorrow; you don't need to worry about it. Tomorrow is not even in our hands. However, there are a lot of predictions about that. Many predicted that California would go under water a long time ago. There are many predictions, but the One who created it all knows when to dissolve it.

Instead of wasting time worrying about these things, accept whatever God sends. Say to yourself, "Today I am here, hail and healthy." Let us do whatever we can to help each other live comfortable and harmonious lives. Today you are in good shape; enjoy that. Be a useful person. If you worry about tomorrow, you have lost today also. A person who worries about tomorrow cannot be happy today. There is a beautiful proverb: "A bird in the hand is worth two in the bush." So, tomorrow is still in the bush; today is in the hand.

So many people want to know what will happen to the world. By worrying about the future, you have literally lost your golden present. Make use of the golden present. Enjoy the golden now. If you're worried about the end of the world, you're missing the present existence of the world. Now it exists, is it not so? It's not yet ended. Are you making use of this world now? No—not if you are worrying about the end. I say: Now you are on sturdy ground. Enjoy it.

If you dwell on what might happen, even before the world shakes, you'll be shaking. Today you are well-grounded. Enjoy the life that's given to you. Don't worry about tomorrow. The people who worry about tomorrow miss today. So, make hay while the sun shines—that's my policy. Take it easy. Never, never give room for any fear. Trust in a higher will. Trust in saintly persons. Trust in great teachers, great masters, great vibrations. They are there to help you, to protect you, to give you fearlessness. Even if you are shaky, remind yourself: "Yes, I'm being taken care of. I am protected." Have that confidence.

Often, our unclean minds don't allow us to be confident. We might go to worship and kneel in front of God and say, "God, you are the Almighty. It's all Thy will. Thy will be done."

But at the same time, our minds are disturbed, thinking, "Oh, I don't know. I'm terribly afraid of what might happen." It's self-contradiction. If you have put yourself in the hands of the Almighty, you should be comfortable here and now. Say, "Yes. I am being taken care of. There's nothing to worry about." Okay?

Never, never, never give up hope. There's always a bright day. There's a great power behind everything. So don't give up. Have that confidence, have that hope. I don't believe in all the doomsday predictions. I consider this a transitory period. We are witnessing a great change. When a seedling is transplanted, at first its leaves wither and fall. It has to face that stage; that's part of the process of getting rooted in the earth. It can't live in the nursery always. In the same way, I see a very bright future for humankind. The positive changes we are seeing are the proof of what is to come.

I really feel we're going to see a better world. If you want to know why I feel this way, it's because I see more and more people wanting to know the truth, becoming interested in Yoga and spirituality and leading more caring and compassionate lives. The consciousness of people is changing, and they want to know how to lead a better life. So, please, have that hope in your heart and that trust that we are building a better world. My prophecy is there is no doomsday. God isn't going to doom anybody's life. It's all going to be great.

All my love and blessings and all my prayers are with you. My prayer is always that universal love will light our paths.

OM Shanti, Shanti, Shanti.

Appendix

Three Easy "Stress Busters"

We have compiled three simple Yoga practices that have been shown to be very effective in reducing stress and promoting ease of body and mind. These practices are part of all Integral Yoga® classes.

Guided Deep Relaxation

Deep relaxation (*Yoga Nidra*) is a simple, yet highly effective technique for putting the body, breath and mind in a state of deep relaxation. You can try this practice of deep relaxation that we hope will help you to get in touch with your own inner peace–the real You. To experience this inner peace, the body, the breath and the mind must all be in harmony. By keeping your thoughts in the here and now, your awareness will become more focused and you will begin to feel more peaceful.

This is done in a natural progression through alternately tensing and relaxing all the muscle groups of the body. As the body becomes more relaxed, the breath and the mind also become more tranquil, allowing you to sink deeper and deeper into your natural state of inner peace.

To prepare for this profound relaxation experience, you'll need to find a clean and quiet place where you can leave all your cares and concerns behind. Lie down on your back on a comfortable but firm mat or on your bed. You're going to have a most beautiful experience, a very deep relaxation. Lying on your back, have your legs about a foot apart. Let your arms be relaxed and about a foot away from your sides, with the palms facing toward the ceiling.

You may now shift your body slightly until you find the position that is absolutely comfortable and most restful for you. If you need to make adjustments—such as a pillow beneath your knees—go ahead and do that before you start the deep relaxation. A modified version of this deep relaxation may also be done while sitting in a chair if you are not able to lie down.

You will purposely be tensing and relaxing each part of the body. You will find that you receive maximum benefit from this if you put all your attention into each part of the body as you tense and relax it. When you raise a part of your body, for example your right arm, raise it slightly–perhaps 6 inches or less. Then after tensing your arm, you just let it fall to the floor as if it were attached to a string held from above, and the string had just been cut. You will do this for each part of the body.

First, have a few slow deep breaths, breathing through your nose. Every time you inhale, feel that you are filling your body with total peace and tranquility. Each time you exhale, feel that you are blowing out all the tension in your body and mind. Inhale fresh cool air. Exhale hot tense air. Then, bring your total awareness to the right leg. Inhale deeply. Tense every muscle in the right leg, raise it a few inches, hold and tense it a little more. And, release the leg and exhale. Gently roll the leg from side to side and then leave it relaxed. Just forget the right leg completely.

Next, bring your awareness to the left leg. Inhale, tensing the leg, lift it slightly. Hold it tight there. You can tighten a little more and release, exhaling. Gently roll it from side to side a few times and leave it relaxed. Now there's no tension anywhere from the hips down to your toes.

Become aware of the buttocks. Tense them; inhale and hold the breath while tensing. Keep tensing and, after a few seconds, let the tension in your buttocks and your inhalation also be suddenly released. Now, think of the abdominal area. Inhale deeply. Imagine that your stomach is like a balloon. Fill it with air and let it expand to its limit. Hold the breath for a few seconds and when you release it, let the air burst out through the mouth.

Now come to the chest area. This time, inhale and fill up the chest. Let your chest expand as much as possible. Hold the breath a few seconds and release.

Next, we move onto the arms. Think of the right arm. Stretch out the right arm; spread out the fingers of your right hand. Tense it. Now make the right hand into a fist. Make it really tight. Inhale and raise the arm slightly. Hold for a second, then release. Gently roll the right arm from side to side and then, with the palm facing the ceiling, let it be. Bring your awareness to the left arm. Stretch out the left arm and spread out the fingers of your left hand. Make the hand into a fist. Make it really tight. Inhale and raise the arm slightly, hold a second and release. Now gently roll the left arm from side to side. Then, with the palm facing the ceiling, let it be.

Become aware of your shoulders. Tighten your shoulders without moving any other part of the body. Let the shoulders be lifted and pulled toward your ears. Hold the shoulders tensed and tight. Release. Once again lift your shoulders and squeeze them tightly. Release. Next is the neck area. Slowly roll the head to the right and then slowly to the left. Do this a few times; and, as you gently roll the head, imagine that you are relaxing each and every muscle in your neck. Now, leave your neck relaxed and head centered.

Now we'll relax the facial muscles. First, open your mouth slightly and stretch the jaw from side to side. Open and close the lower jaw and move it around. Now leave it relaxed. Press the lips together tightly. And relax. Now tense and wrinkle the nose. Relax. Next, close the eyes and tightly squeeze your eyes and forehead. Relax. We will relax all these muscles once more by now tightening all the muscles in your face, squeezing them into a tight, prune face. Squeeze more and relax.

We have literally relaxed all the muscles of the body. Let's check once more for any remaining tension. Without moving any part of the body, just mentally review each part, starting from the toes and moving upward, part by part. Through the lower legs and now the upper legs. If you become aware of any tension in any part, mentally repeat the word "relax" and feel the tension slip away. Continue by mentally checking the buttocks, the abdomen, the chest, the lower back, the upper back. Now check the hands and the arms, the shoulders and the back of the neck, the face and finally, the top of the head.

The entire body is now completely relaxed. Your muscles are so relaxed that they may not even want to move. This is the state of deep relaxation. Take this moment to experience how totally relaxed and peaceful your body feels. Because of the total relaxation of the body, you do not need to breathe heavily. Your breathing, is in fact, naturally very shallow. So simply become aware of the breath. See how calm it is as it flows in and out, gently and rhythmically. You have forgotten the body and are thinking of the breath.

Now, forget even the breath. You are entering an even deeper state of relaxation. Bring your awareness now to the mind. You will see that even the mind is very calm and quiet. Just allow the mind to rest. Let the mind sink into a still deeper state of rest and peace. If any thoughts come that try and pull you from the here and now, do not get involved with them. Watch them come, and watch them go.

As the mind rests, the breath is calm and the body totally relaxed. You are able to transcend the body, breath and mind now. You are in a transcendental state of profound peace and relaxation. Realize that this peace that you experience as you sink deeper still into total tranquility is your True Nature. Remain in your True Nature for awhile. Enjoy this Supreme Peace. This is the real you. This is Self-realization.

As you come out of this state of relaxation you will retain this experience of inner peace. The body and mind will feel totally new, totally fresh and filled with health and vitality. Take time to come out of this deep relaxation. Notice that your breathing is very, very slow. Now, begin to make the breath a little deeper. Slowly inhale and exhale, becoming more and more conscious of the breath. Make the breathing deeper still. As you inhale, feel that fresh energy, vital energy, is flowing all through the veins, all through your body–from head to foot. This energy is energizing and awakening the entire body part by part.

As the energy flows, you will begin to feel a slight tingling sensation all over the face and then through the torso. Feel it moving through the arms. Feel the entire body begin to be awakened by this flow of fresh energy. Allow the energy to flow into your legs. You are able to feel the fresh energy, flowing and surging all over the body. You can begin to move the body, by stretching gently. Feel the freshness and vitality of the body. You can now slowly and gently get up and face the day with a renewed sense of peace.

Health, not disease, is your birthright; strength not weakness is your heritage; courage not sorrow; peace not restlessness; knowledge not ignorance. May you attain this birthright, this divine heritage, to shine as fully developed Yogis, radiating joy, peace and knowledge everywhere. OM Shanti Shanti Shanti.

–Sri Swami Satchidananda

Three-part Deep Breathing

Calm the breath, you have calmed the mind.

–Sri Swami Satchidananda

If you observe your breathing during times of stress and agitation, you may notice that it's shallow and rapid. One of the best tools we have to help us relax during these times is as close as our own breath. In fact, it is our own breath. *Pranayama*, the practice of breathing techniques, is a vital and important part of the science of Yoga. *Pranayama* helps to clear, calm and center the mind and emotions. There are several wonderful breathing practices, and we are offering one of them below.

Deergha Swasam, deep three-part breathing, is the most basic *pranayama* practice. It can be done anywhere, any time. Even doing this for a few moments can dramatically help one to relax and, then, meet a situation with more clarity.

The full use of the diaphragm, achieved by slow even deep breathing, leads to relaxation of other parts of the body and to a calm, relaxed state of mind. We will learn this part by part.

Preparation: Sit in a comfortable cross-legged position with the spine erect, but not stiff, shoulders back, head centered, chin level and eyes closed. If you're unable to sit in this posture, you may sit on a firm, supportive chair. If you're sitting in a chair, be sure your feet touch the ground and that you are able to sit with your spine erect and straight. If you have a disability or illness that keeps you from sitting comfortably, it is fine to lie down on as firm a surface as possible.

To begin the first part: Without disturbing the rest of the body, take your right hand and place it on the abdomen. Observe how the right hand rises and falls, as the breath comes in and out of the body. Observe, as you inhale, that the abdomen expands slightly and with the exhalation, it contracts. The inhalation is like a balloon filling with air; and, on the exhalation the abdomen contracts and the balloon collapses. Now very gently, as you begin to exhale, apply a gentle pressure on the abdomen with the hand. Push the abdomen all the way in as the air goes out; then, relaxing the abdomen, allow the air to flow in. Gently press down as the air goes out, and release the hand as the air comes in. Do this a few times. After the next exhalation, allow the breath to return to normal.

For the second part of the three-part breath, allow the right hand to remain on the abdomen and take the left hand and place it on the lower chest, right below the breastbone. You'll see that these two hands move independently of each other. With the right hand pushing down gently on the abdomen, exhale and now inhale, feeling the abdomen expand as the right hand comes up.

Now, allow the breath to also fill the lower chest. As the breath moves up and the lower chest expands, the left hand rises. On the exhalation, feel the left hand fall and then the right hand fall. Continue with an inhalation, observing the right hand coming up and the left hand also coming up. Exhale and observe the left hand going down followed by the right hand going down.

Continue these two parts, each one flowing into the other, but independently moving. Inhale filing the abdomen, and then continue to inhale, filling the lower chest. Exhale, emptying the lower chest, and then the abdomen gently contracts. Now, inhale fully, allowing the abdomen to expand, and continue to fill the lower lungs, bringing in fresh oxygen. Expand the rib cage to the fullest capacity, but without straining. Next, exhale and allow the breath to return to normal and relax.

Now you can begin to learn the third part of the three-part breathing. This involves a slight rising of the collarbones to completely fill the apex of the lungs. So, exhale, bringing in the abdomen. Then inhale, expanding the abdomen; the lower chest expands, and now the breath comes all the way up so that the collarbones rise slightly. Exhale and allow the collarbones to fall. The lower chest now gently contracts as it empties.

Finally, contract the abdomen. Expand the abdomen as you inhale, filling and expanding the lower chest and then the upper chest so the collarbones slightly rise. Now exhale and feel the collarbones fall, the lower chest contract and the abdomen contract. Continue a few more rounds of this three-part breath at your own pace. You should begin to feel a gentle flow between the three parts.

Observe the breath in its stillness and calmness and notice how relaxed this makes you feel.

OM Shanti Meditation

Meditation is a beautiful way to find serenity and focus in daily life and, certainly, in times of distress. The aim of meditation is to calm and center the mind. A mantra can help to focus the mind. Many mantras include *OM*. In the beginning, God, or the Cosmic Consciousness, expressed as the Word or as vibration. That vibration produced a hum, which gave rise to the syllable *OM*. *Shanti* is the Sanskrit word for peace.

By concentrating on this inner vibration, you tune in to the cosmic sound. You will feel peaceful and blissful because you are going to the very source of your True Nature. Repetition of this mantra truly brings an experience of peace within. By remaining in this state of peace, you will also be able to send out powerful peace vibrations that will travel to all those in need all over the globe.

This practice can be combined with the three-part breathing described on the previous pages. Sit comfortably with the entire weight of the body supported by the straight spine.

Observe your breathing, slowly making it deeper and deeper. Take long, slow deep three-part breaths, carefully observing the flow of the air in and out. Follow the breath as it goes in. Feel that as you inhale, you are breathing in ease and peace. As you exhale, you're releasing any stress or tension. After doing this a few times, let the breath flow in and out by itself without using any force. After watching the breath for a few minutes, mentally repeat *OM* with the next incoming breath; and, when it goes out, mentally repeat *Shanti*.

Don't consciously control the breathing, but just be conscious of the breath and combine it with *OM Shanti*. Imagine the air flows in saying *OM* and rolls out with *Shanti*. You need not keep repeating it now; just feel it. If the mind wanders, gently bring it back to rest on your focus of concentration. If you watch carefully, you will not only feel the air saying the mantra; but you'll find that you can listen to it also. That needs complete attention, an indrawn mind. Throughout this meditation, keep the spine erect so that the flow will be easy. Let the *OM* breath continue to bring a deep sense of peace and relaxation into your body and mind; then, with *Shanti*, let any and all tension be exhaled and released.

Carry this peaceful feeling from meditation all through the day, all through the week. Carry it all through your life. Even in the midst of a busy life, you can retain this peace. Learn to do that; then, it will make no difference whether you are in a church or a stock market. You can be in peace, at ease. Then, it's only a matter of expanding–it's limitless. May this peace and joy prevail in your life always.

–Sri Swami Satchidananda

You might find that further instruction is helpful as you learn these techniques. For instructional books and CDs, please contact Shakticom: 1-800-476-1347 or www.shakticom.org. To locate an Integral Yoga teacher in your area, consult the Integral Yoga Teachers directory on the Integral Yoga Teachers Association website: www.iyta.org.

Sri Swami Satchidananda

Sri Swami Satchidananda was one of the first Yoga masters to bring the classical Yoga tradition to the West. He taught Yoga postures to Americans, introduced them to meditation, a vegetarian diet and a more compassionate lifestyle.

During this period of cultural awakening, iconic pop artist Peter Max and a small circle of his artist friends beseeched the Swami to extend his brief stop in New York City so they could learn from him the secret of finding physical, mental and spiritual health, peace and enlightenment.

Three years later, he led some half a million American youth in chanting *OM*, when he delivered the official opening remarks at the 1969 Woodstock Music and Art Festival and he became known as "the Woodstock Guru."

The distinctive teachings he brought with him blend the physical discipline of Yoga, the spiritual philosophy of Vedantic literature and the interfaith ideals he pioneered.

These techniques and concepts influenced a generation and spawned a Yoga culture that is flourishing today. Today, over twenty million Americans practice Yoga as a means for managing stress, promoting health, slowing down the aging process and creating a more meaningful life.

The teachings of Swami Satchidananda have spread into the mainstream and thousands of people now teach Yoga. Integral Yoga is the foundation for Dr. Dean Ornish's landmark work in reversing heart disease and Dr. Michael Lerner's noted Commonweal Cancer Help program.

Today, Integral Yoga Institutes, teaching centers and certified teachers throughout the United States and abroad offer classes and training programs in all aspects of Integral Yoga.

In 1979, Sri Swamiji was inspired to establish Satchidananda Ashram–Yogaville. Based on his teachings, it is a place where people of different faiths and backgrounds can come to realize their essential oneness.

One of the focal points of Yogaville is the Light Of Truth Universal Shrine (LOTUS). This unique interfaith shrine honors the Spirit that unites all the world religions, while celebrating their diversity. People from all over the world come there to meditate and pray.

Over the years, Sri Swamiji received many honors for his public service, including the Juliet Hollister Interfaith Award presented at the United Nations and in 2002 the U Thant Peace Award.

In addition, he served on the advisory boards of many Yoga, world peace and interfaith organizations. He is the author of many books on Yoga and is the subject of the documentary, *Living Yoga: The life and teachings of Swami Satchidananda.*

In 2002, he entered *Mahasamadhi* (a God-realized soul's conscious final exit from the body).

For more information, visit: www.swamisatchidananda.org